LORD, HELP ME!...

THE DESPERATE DIETER

BETH HAMMOND

Concordia

Publishing House
St. Louis

Concordia Publishing House, St. Louis, Missouri
Copyright ©1983 Concordia Publishing House
Manufactured in the United States of America

Library of Congress Cataloging in Publication Data

Hammond, Beth.
    Lord, help me!

    1. Reducing diets. 2. Reducing — Prayer-books and
devotions — English. I. Title
RM222.2.H225 1983   613.2'5'019   82-23669
ISBN 0-570-03896-0

1 2 3 4 5 6 7 8 9 10   PP   92 91 90 89 88 87 86 85 84 83

With Love
to Nicholas, Staci, and Bill

Contents

Shakespeare's Hamlet cried: "Oh, that this too too solid flesh would melt, thaw and resolve itself into a dew!" Many an overweight person has echoed that plea, as does Beth Hammond when she prays, "Lord, help me!"

Millions of Americans, including Christians, and especially women, are struggling with the besetting problem of overweight. They range from the compulsive nibbler to the compulsive overeater. If the problem is organic/physical, a physician should advise and help. But there is another, additional resource that Beth Hammond turns to: prayer to a God who cares for all His children, fat or thin.

Readers will identify with Beth as she looks at her situation subjectively and objectively, sometimes close to despair, and at other times taking a relaxed and hopeful view of life that can be rewarding and useful on the way to the ideal figure. She tries to begin with a healthy outlook as she heads for a healthy body. The struggling reader is invited to share the trip.

If Paul Could Do It, I Can

I'm weak, Jesus, I admit it.
I can identify with Your apostle Paul,
 who was not reluctant to confess:
 "Who is weak, and I am not weak?"
Realizing his weakness, he nevertheless said:
 "I can do all things in Him [Christ]
 who strengthens me."
If it were not for that promise of potential success,
 Paul would have quit any number of times.
And so would I.
It's because of You, my Savior and my Lord,
 that I can reasonably expect victory
 in this daily struggle.
You are with me to strengthen and uphold me,
 to accept and encourage me.
You can keep me from making an idol
 of thinness as much as of food.
You will continue to accept me as I am,
 fat or thin—the person inside this
 envelope of flesh.
I will live each day in that acceptance.
Thank You for Your kind of love,
 Christ, my Lord.
Through You I can do all things,
 even this.
Amen.

Desperation

Lord, please!
I don't want to be fat!
Hear my cry, my plea of desperation.
You can work miracles, Lord.
Take this weight from me,
  and let me wake up tomorrow
  25 pounds thinner.
God, please! I hate myself.
It is agony to live under a burden of fat.
I don't know if I can endure, Lord.
No one loves me or even cares.
How could they when I'm so fat?
Who can know the torture that grips my soul,
  the pain that tears at my innermost being?
I feel so unworthy.
I feel less than human.
Lord, please, make me stop eating.
I would give almost anything to lose weight.
Lord, don't you have a miracle for me?
I feel such hopelessness, such despair.
Depression sits on me as though I were
  its personal easy chair.
Diets are slow and painful,
  and I don't tolerate pain well.
It hurts every fiber of my body
  not to eat something I want.
Nothing but food seems to satisfy these cravings,
  but then that moment comes
  when there is nothing more to eat,
  and all the bad feelings

come rushing back even stronger,
demanding more food to pacify them.
Lord, You can help.
Lift my desperation.
Help me overcome the feelings
of inadequacy and self-hate
without abusing food.
Make me aware of what I am doing
and give me patience.
I know there is no 48-hour cure for overweight,
as much as I passionately desire one.
Lord, give me the strength to lose weight
just a pound at a time—an ounce at a time.
Let me stop blaming myself
and love myself once again.
I'm beginning to lose weight.
I realize I will have to struggle, Lord.
I need Your power
to meet this struggle victoriously.
Stay with me, Lord, and give me courage.
With You, I can do it.
Please, Lord, let me be slim.
In Jesus' name. Amen.

Lord,
Do You know what it's like?
    Can You imagine being fat?
Fat is avoiding mirrors
    and being afraid of the scale.
Fat is being ignored when you want to be noticed
    and noticed when you prefer oblivion.
Fat is eating because you want so desperately
    to lose weight.
Fat is not buying new clothes because you're afraid
    the salesgirl might see what size you wear.
Fat is feeling:
    feeling stared at, feeling sorry for yourself,
    feeling angry, inferior, scared, shy, embarrassed,
    abused, scorned, depressed, alone, tired, confused,
    feeling every torrent of emotion except jolly.
Fat is denying you feel anything but jolly.
Fat is a terrible place to visit
    and a prison to live in.
Fat is crying over spilled milk weeks later.
Fat is expecting to fail,
    not believing in yourself,
    because if you can't do a "simple" thing
    like lose a few pounds,
    how can you accomplish anything else?
Fat is resentment and despair.
Lord, fat is crying out to You in a wilderness
    and feeling even You won't hear.
Lord, touch me and tell me that You care,
    and that You love me.
Amen.

Denial

Now, Lord,
You really don't think I'm *that* fat!
Sure, I *could* stand to lose a few pounds,
        but a diet isn't really *that* important.
Besides, today doesn't really count
        because tomorrow I'm going to be very careful
        about what I eat.
What's a couple of pounds?
When the first of the month gets here,
        I'll go on a strict diet
        and lose 10 or 15 pounds.
I might even do a few sit-ups
        to make sure I lose in the right places.
Anyway, what difference does it make?
My weight and eating habits
        don't hurt anybody.
I feel a little depressed about it sometimes,
but it's not like indulging in addictions
        that hurt the people around you.
Although stuffing does sometimes make me drowsy
        and not quite as alert,
        I won't go out and have a car wreck
        from eating too much.
And it is *my* problem.
I don't hurt my family or friends
        by eating too much.

Lord, are You speaking to me again?
You are saying that intemperance with food
        is dulling the richness of my life?

14 My family and friends *are* hurt
　　by my overindulgence?
I guess I haven't noticed
　　how food-centered I have become.
This overweight, overeating regimen
　　does cause hurt and pain—to me and my family.
Lord, help me to stop denying that I have a problem.
I need to look within myself and see myself
　　as I really am.
Give me self-knowledge to fight overeating.
This is the moment I can start rewriting my past
　　so I can look back at my life with pride
　　instead of guilt and shame.
As I control my eating and my appearance this moment,
　　I become more at peace with myself
　　and I gain the pride and respect of those who love
　　me.
How can any food compete with inner peace?
How can any taste delight compare with the respect
　　of my family and friends?
With this perspective and Your help, Lord,
　　I will cease denying my problems,
　　I will defeat the taste temptations,
　　and I will be a person
　　I can love.
Amen.

Why?

Why, Father,
Why is it so hard to diet and so easy to gain weight?
Why does being overweight make me suffer so when it
    doesn't seem to bother some people?
Why can't I be like my pretty friends, my slim friends?
You supposedly want the best for each of us;
    then why did you make me fat?
How am I supposed to love, honor, and worship a God
    who would cause me to suffer this affliction?

Lord, I'm sorry!
When my soul is touched and crushed
    by the despair I feel from my weight,
    I lash out at whatever is near —
    at my family, at myself, and even at You.
I strike and pacify myself simultaneously by eating.
I touch the bottom of my emotional pit
    under the burden of my weight.
Lord, I cry to You for answers to my whys.
I feel so emotionally lost and long to be found
    and folded in security.
If dieting can't be easy, Lord,
    strengthen me so that I can
    cope with the difficulties.
Teach me that I am not a sole sufferer.
Help me tune in to the pains of those around me,
    and offer soothing balm and understanding.
Even if everyone I see about me is thin,
    and I am fat,
    give the courage to rejoice in their thinness,
    not begrudge it.

16   I know You do want what is best for me, Lord.
      You didn't make me fat—
            my own guilt, pride, gluttony, lust for food,
            ego, and selfishness have done that.
      You are here to stand by me and support me.
      With You, I am overcoming the enemies within me
            that once led me to gorge myself with food.
      I will be thin, Lord.
      I will be thin.
      Amen.

Facing the Day

Lord,
Fresh morning has washed the land.
Now is the time for new beginnings.
I feel renewed strength, but still I fear.
Will my strength be sufficient
      to meet the needs of today?
Please, Father,
Stay with me throughout this day.
Help me choose my foods and eat in a way
      that will please You.
Excuses to eat come so easily.
Sharpen my awareness and help me defeat the excuses
      that tempt me today.
With Your help I will focus my attention
      on the beautiful and important things in life
      and concentrate, not on eating
      but on being the best person
      I can be.
Thank You, Father.
Amen.

Reawaken My Senses

Father,
In everything I see Your hand and Your love.
I have senses to see, hear, touch, smell, and taste.
I glorify Your works.
But my values have become misplaced, Lord.
The senses You gave me to enjoy
  the bounty of the earth,
   I have trained to adore food.
I have failed to lift up my eyes to the hills
  because they have been focused on food.
I have not heard Your voice,
  as I have listened to my inner cries
  of "Eat, eat!"
I have not touched the wind,
  for my fingers have been too busy
  with food preparation and eating.
My nose has become deadened
  to all but the aromas of food.
Taste is almost ignored in my eagerness to indulge.
Lord, forgive me and reawaken my senses.
Touch my eyes and let them behold
  the beauty of the earth.
Open my ears to Your voice.
Let my touch explore the grandeur of Your world
  and my nose find the sweet scent of life.
As I learn to eat wisely,
  teach me a discerning taste,
I sing Your praise, Father!
Amen.

My Food, My God

Father,
Today I made a discovery.
When I pray I use Your name,
    but my true god has been food.
I have placed food at the center of my universe,
    above all else.
My life structure has been determined
    by places and times to eat.
When I wake in the morning,
    I turn not to You but to my coffeepot, moaning,
    "I'm nothing until I have that first cup of coffee."
How, Lord, can I overcome
    this demon that controls me?
What a price I have paid for making food my god!
I have become completely unaware
    of the blessings You have given.
My talents are buried under a layer of fat
    and years of disuse.
Please, God, forgive me and help me.
My spirit is ready.
I don't want my epitaph to read:
    "All she did was eat."
Help me change.
Father, You have given me a gift of awareness—
    a glimpse of myself as a food-oriented person.
By the power of Your Holy Spirit
    I will use this knowledge to change
    and to uncover and utilize
    the talents I have unconsciously buried
    through years of excessive eating
    and indulging.

My universe
    will no longer revolve around food.
(Didn't our Lord Jesus say,
    "Do not be anxious about…what you shall eat…"?)
Thank You for the courage and presence of mind
    to fight my food obsession
        until it is gone.
Amen.

Tears

Lord,
I cry when I diet.
The unfairness of the necessity to diet
    overwhelms me.
Why should *I* have this problem?
I want to eat all those nice things
    it seems everybody else eats —
        but I want to be thin.

Lord, You could make me slender
and still allow me to eat.
Why do I have to be the one to gain
when I look at food?
Lord, I'm sorry!
Let me feel Your presence and listen.
My lesson is responsibility.
Lord—how often I have willfully
chosen irresponsibility!
Over and over again
I tempt myself with irresistibles
and succumb to morsel after morsel.
By my own hand I have become overweight.
Responsibility is a hard lesson, Lord.
It means caring for my body
and developing proper eating habits.
Help me build on the groundwork
of my successes, Father.
As I continue to grow
in learning control and responsibility,
my tears will cease.
Thank You, Father, for Your guidance.
Amen.

Escape

Lord,
My whole body aches with the loneliness
of a prisoner confined to a windowed cell,
where he can see freedom
but cannot touch it himself.

Fat is my constant companion,
    a specter haunting my every emotion,
    kibitzing my every activity.
I want to lose it,
    but I don't know how to live without it.
I don't know how to be thin—
    how to eat, dress, or live like a thin person
But I've learned every corridor
    of the maze of fat.
Every door in this prison
    is locked by an unhappy key,
    a key of loneliness, anger, depression.
I know how to live in these walls,
    and I'm miserable here.
Lord, please release me from this prison
    I've built around myself.
Help me find the key marked "Escape."
Lead me through the tangled, twisted passageways
    to an exit.
Lord, I'm ready to stop compensating
    and making excuses,
I'm ready to step into the freedom of thinness.
Grant me the bravery and courage
    to leave my companion fat
    and face the world as I become a thin being.
Thank You, Father.
Amen.

Lord,
Each day I delay
    adds one more day of being fat to my life.
Since I was young,
    I have wanted to be slim and attractive.
Now I have lived nearly one-third of my life,
    and almost every single day
    I have found an excuse not to diet, or to cheat.
It's only after all this time I've learned
    no one can lose weight tomorrow.
Years of "I'll diet tomorrow"
    have written for me a fat past
    with chapters of miseries.
I want to come in from the fat—
    step out of my bittersweet cloudy coverings
    into the sunshine of life.
In the future I want to be able to pause again
    to assess my existence,
    to speak of a time in my life
    when I made a decision
    to be true to myself, and take control.
Help me take that step now, Lord,
    and change the pattern
    in the loom that weaves my life.
I could diet "tomorrow" for the rest of my life
    and always be fat,
    but because I walk with You, Lord,
    I will diet only today and be thin.
Today determines how my autobiography will read,
Together we can write each line with pride.
Amen.

Like a Tree

Father,
I open my curtains to the morning
    and expose the rich freshness of a new day.
I watch the trees reaching for Your sunshine.
They bathe themselves in its glorious,
    life-giving brilliance.
Their leaves are cupped
    to catch the droplets of dew
    vaporizing from a cloudless sky.
Each tree stretches its branches,
    filling itself with Your love
    and spreading that love to the winds.
Lord, let me be like a tree.
I will reach for what I need for growth and health.
I will enjoy the natural grains and foods
    You have created for the nurture of my body.
I will appreciate the blessing of water
    that comes directly from the heavens
    to satisfy my thirst.
I will stretch and exercise my body,
    filling it with Your love.
I will spread Your love in my world.
The psalmist said, "He shall be like a tree."
Let me be like that tree
    as I step into this new day.
Amen.

As a Christian

Lord God,
I cannot be a food-worshiper
    and truly call myself a Christian.
I must put no other gods before You.
I often look smugly around at those
    who place money and possessions
    before their love of You,
    or those who seek physical pleasures and thrills,
    or the people who always have
    something better to do on Sunday
    than to give You a few minutes of their time.
But I, Lord, am guilty of this same sin.
While I condemn others,
    I continue to glorify food.
"You shall love the Lord your God
    with all your heart...soul...mind...strength,"
    Jesus said.
My heart, mind, and strength are focused on food.
I'm afraid I worship food, Lord, instead of You.
Please, Father, forgive me.
With the help of Your Holy Spirit, Father,
    I will focus on You.
I turn over to You this demon
    of overeating and food-centeredness
    that has crept into my life.
I will be a consistent Christian,
    and food will take a proper perspective
    in my life.
Your light will shine through me,
    no longer dimmed by layers of fat.
My witness will be of joy and peace within myself.
Amen.

Before
Shopping for Groceries

Lord,
Sometimes I think it would be easier to walk through
      the valley of the shadow
      than to walk through the aisles of the grocery store.
I am tempted at every turn.
My eyes delight in the bright packagings.
Pictures of delicacies and delights in cellophane
      seduce my will.
I don't want to leave the tempting assortment
      on the shelves.
And, if I succumb and allow the teasing temptations
      to slink and slither into my cart,
      I can hardly wait to get past the cashier
      so I can open my treasures.
Some have never made it home.
In my lust I have had packages opened
      and nearly half-devoured
      before even starting my car.
Father, take my hand and walk these aisles with me.
Give me vision to see through the glitter.
Give me wisdom to select my purchases carefully.
With these gifts, as I walk these aisles,
      I know I will also be blessed
      with relaxation and peace of mind.
Thank You, Father, for vision, wisdom,
      and the knowledge of Your presence.
Amen.

Lord,
I can't deny my children.
You know how important it is
    for children to feel loved.
It wouldn't be right to deny them
    just because I'm on a diet.
They are growing so rapidly.
A few snacks now and then won't hurt them and are
    good for energy.
Lord, I've actually convinced myself this is true.
    I actually believe
    I bring home *my* favorite goodies for the kids.
I have assured myself
    that these snacks are good for my children,
    that the goodies will not slow them
    into a sugar stupor
    or make them hyper or fat.
    (They shouldn't —
    I eat 90 percent of what I buy "for the kids."
Lord, buying my no-nos for the kids
    is an enormously lame excuse.
They *don't* need
    extra-refined sugars and starches in their diets,
    and those empty calories *could* do them much harm.
If I'm honest,
    I must acknowledge that if given a choice,
    my kids will usually choose an apple or banana
    over a sugared snack.
My children need a good balance
    of hugs, kind words, and attention,
    not unbalanced calories.

It is important for children to feel loved,
    but *love is not food.*
Help me to treat myself and my children
    with true *love.*
Amen.

Before Preparing a Meal

Lord,
Here I am in my kitchen.
You have helped me select my menu wisely.
Now I must prepare it.
Please be with me and help me feel Your presence
    as I ready this meal.
With You, Father, I can be prepared
    for the familiar temptations of cooking
    and overcome them.

28 With Your strength, I can avoid the seemingly innocent
        tasting that would sneak added flab onto this body
        You have put in my care.
Because You care, Lord,
        I can busy my hands
        with the details of making a lovely meal.
I can occupy my mind with positive thoughts.
My appetite and senses
        will not be dulled and deadened
        by bits slipping through my lips.
My self-esteem will be intact.
I will be able to appreciate my meal
        with the full value of the senses You have given me.
Stay by me, Father.
Amen.

Married

Father,
I feel if I truly love and care for my spouse,
        I must keep my body in the best possible condition.
Married, I find myself involved
        in more eating situations
        such as his Christmas party,
        extra dinners and social events,
        and extra eating cues
        such as when he decides it's time for a nibble.
Many of these are situations that cannot be avoided.
Learning to cope with additional food stimulation
        is extremely difficult.
I must solve the weight problems
        that tie in with marriage.

Lead me to the solution, Father.
My husband loves me.
I don't need to impress him with high-caloric foods.
He will be just as impressed
    by a carefully planned meal
    designed to keep us both thin and healthy.
If I serve him with care,
    he will know he is loved.
Father, a beautiful thing like marriage
    should not be turned into an excuse
    for unwanted weight gain.
Keep me alert, Father,
    and sensitive to the needs of my marriage.
Help me to satisfy these needs,
    not with food but with Your gifts
    of understanding, creativity, and love.
Amen.

Before Eating a Meal

Lord,
Your blessings are so bountiful!
I usually consider only the food
    when praising Your blessings.
Help me remember that temperance
    is also Your blessing.
Help me to claim the richness
    of the blessing of moderation
    for myself.
For when I do not abuse Your gift of food
    by overindulgence,
    I become stronger—

30 physically, emotionally, and spiritually.
My physical self is strengthened
by not having the burden
of extra calories, carbohydrates, and fats.
My emotional self is strengthened
because I am in control
and am not burdened by the guilt and remorse
of letting food be stronger than I.
And my spiritual self is strengthened
because in accepting Your gift of temperance,
I know I please You and do not abuse
the body You have put in my keeping.
Help me to stay aware of all these things, Lord,
as I eat this meal and enjoy it
in the quantities required
for proper maintenance of my body.
Amen.

Before Taking Seconds

Lord,
You have blessed me with a good meal.
I appreciate the bounty You have given me.
But my taste buds have been teased.
I don't want to stop eating.
I want more food.
Father, help me consider my needs.
If I can say honestly that I need it,
then allow me to take more without guilt.
But, Father, if my desire for more
is a lustful desire,

please give me the courage to admit this to myself
and the strength to leave the food on the table.
I want to learn to eat,
    not as a glutton but as Your child.
Give me Your blessing, Lord.
Amen.

Leftovers

Lord,
Leftovers are my downfall.
Because people are starving,
    I am plagued with guilt
    if I even think about throwing away food.
However, I admit it doesn't bother me
    to throw away leftovers I don't like;
    and, if my concern is so great,
    why haven't I learned to cook
    in nutritionally adequate quantities?
Even so, I don't think my concern
    is just another excuse to eat, Lord.
I feel real empathy.
When full and comfortable, I think of someone
    who may have been lucky
    to have had a slice of bread.
This is a problem
    I haven't been able to resolve, Father.
I don't understand why some have to starve
    and others of us are easily able
    to eat ourselves into oblivion.
I have never experienced real hunger.

If I had, I would probably appreciate
the joy of eating in normal amounts.
When there are leftovers despite careful planning,
I need to learn to throw them away
without guilt.
Eating them detracts from both my health
and appearance.
Help me to keep my compassion
for Your starving peoples,
and to channel that compassion
into constructive tasks
that will aid the hungry.
Thank You, Father, for the bounty given me.
Give me also the gift
of using these blessings wisely.
Amen.

Company

Lord,
It's me again, Your favorite dieter.
I have another problem
that I need help with — company.
My family will be visiting here
for the next two weeks.
I can't serve them my diet foods
or my diet portions,
What is there to do with my diet meals?
How dull!
No one has ever written a book
of 101 ways to serve carrot or celery sticks.

It's a real temptation
    to let my diet go for that short two weeks
    and create delicious, delectable,
    mouth-watering, irresistible dishes.
Company is such a good excuse for a diet break.
But I can't use that excuse.
I can't go off my diet for two weeks.
I could regain as much as ten pounds
    the first week alone—
    then be stuck with that ten pounds
    for the next six months!
My family loves me.
If I explain carefully that I am dieting
for my health and well-being,
they will support me.
They might even join me!
Help me, Lord, not to covet the food
    of the nondieters.
Help me to use our mealtime as family time,
    catching up on special happenings and sharing
    love, rather than concentrating on what
    everybody else is eating.
Help me to remain, Lord,
    Your conscientious dieter.
Amen.

When Tired of Dieting

O Lord,
Sometimes I get so tired of dieting.
I feel so put-upon, so cursed.
Why can't I eat unabashedly?
Lord, *it isn't fair!*
Lord, I feel no condemnation from You
     for my self-pity—only love and compassion.
I know You've promised to give me
       no temptation too great to overcome,
       but overcoming the temptation of food is so painful
It hurts in my gut, my emotions, and my head.
Lord, it's so easy to make excuses,
       so easy to give in,
       so easy to justify just one bite of this,
       one bite of that.
Lord, please refresh my enthusiasm for dieting today.
I won't be concerned about tomorrow
     if You'll just help me through today, Lord.
Renew my energy.
I praise You, Lord, for the strength to fight against
     giving up and giving in.
I praise You for the joy and blessings
     of meeting and overcoming temptation.
Amen.

Celebration

I praise You, Lord!
My diet is working.
My energy level is high.
I have enthusiasm for life.
Keep Your Spirit flowing through me, Lord.
With Your blessings and love,
    I am becoming healthier, move vibrant
      and more alive.
To You, Lord, I raise my voice
      and shout Your praise.
Gloria! Amen.

When Showing
a Loss on the Scale

Lord,
I'm in danger again.
Please, take my hand.
You see, I stepped on the scale
      and my weight is down.
This is a critical time, Lord.
In the past I have often "eased up" a bit on my diet
      because a pound is gone — and suddenly
      I'm no longer dieting.
Please help me not to turn this blessing
      into a weak excuse to break training.

Help this weight loss to bolster
my enthusiasm for the diet,
remembering that working
to mold and keep my body in its healthiest shape
is pleasing to me and to You, Father.
Amen.

When Showing a Gain on the Scale

Oh no, I gained a pound!
I might as well give up today
and start again tomorrow.

Lord,
What am I thinking?
Don't let me give that pound the power to control me
and throw me off my diet.
Help me remember I can never diet tomorrow.
I can only diet today.
So help me, Lord.
Give me the strength I need to diet just for today.
I turn over to You, Lord,
the temptation to procrastinate,
to put off till tomorrow,
and take Your blessing
of being able to diet just for today.
Together, today, we will fight that new pound,
and we will win!
Thank You, Lord.

When Exercise Is Not Appealing

Lord,
Please forgive my apathy,
    but I am overwhelmed
    at the thought of exercise.
My whole body rebels against being moved.
I realize what I really want
    is permanent thinness and attractiveness
    without having to make a personal investment.
But there is a price tag
    on good health and appearance.
In my case, the price is proper diet and exercise.
It is a fair price, a bargain really.
So why do I have such trouble paying what I owe?
Lord, renew my spirit and my outlook.
Help me to appreciate the fact
    that I am able to exercise.
Father, keep me from using exercise
    as an excuse for abusing eating later on.
Grant me the gift of renewed enthusiasm
    and let me feel Your strength.
Thank You, Father.
Amen.

When Tired

Dear God, I'm tired.
I think a quick snack would really pick me up.
Whoops, Lord, I have an excuse to eat.
And it's so easy to give in to an excuse
    when I'm tired.
Lord, help me see that eating now
    would only lead to depression later
    and make it easier to give in
    to other excuses to eat.
Help me find constructive ways
    to renew my body and spirit.
Help me find rest in a nap or a quiet project,
    or a pick-me-up in a brief exercise session.
Give me the strength, Lord,
    to get beyond this tiredness in a constructive way,
    to use this tiredness, not as an excuse for a binge,
    but as an enriching experience.
I praise You, Lord, for guidance and renewed energy.
Amen.

When Sick

Lord,
I feel terrible.
I keep thinking how certain foods
    would soothe the waves in my raging stomach
    or cool the fire in my throat.
Eating would surely ease the pounding in my head.

I shouldn't have to fight temptation
    with my strength sapped by illness.
I can always resume dieting when I feel better.
The path of binging glitters.
Lord, please help me fight the excuses.
If I were to give in now,
    I would not be pampering myself;
    I'd be punishing myself for being sick.
I would have that terrible, painful struggle
    to begin dieting again.
And I would have to recover
    not only from my illness
    but also from the guilt
    that results from cheating.
However, the path of binging still glitters.
Help me see beyond the glitter, Lord.
Keep me true to my diet, to myself, and to You.
Amen.

When Angry

Dear God, I'm mad!
Why do people treat me this way?
All I can think about is getting even.
And I'm hungry.
I'm used to venting my anger with food,
    gnawing and gnashing
    the hunks of stuff into my mouth,
    but I know now I cannot do that
    and please You, Lord.

40   I know I cannot keep this anger and please You.
With the insight You have granted,
    I realize that my anger
    in not correcting the situation
    but *is* hurting me.
I feel bad.
My emotions are twisted
    like children's pipe cleaners after play.
My stomach feels bound and knotted
    by thick, heavy ropes.
My concentration is destroyed
    by the constant throbbing of my anger.
Show me, Lord, a way to purge my body
    of this anger which threatens to destroy me,
    a way to release this emotion I have embraced.
If I am honest with You and myself,
    I know I have chosen to be angry.
With Your help I can equally
    choose freedom from anger.
You have commanded me to forgive others, Father.
Now I see that this is necessary
    more for my sake than for theirs.
Lord, You sent Your Son Jesus to die
    for the sin of anger.
I turn my anger over to You
    and seek Your Spirit's power
    of love and forgiveness,
    and the healing of my wounded spirit.
Amen.

When Depressed

O Lord,
I feel like everyone and everything is against me.
Eating is so comforting.
I can lose my depression in the warm glow of food.
Food smoothes it over, and transports my mind
        away from my worries and woes.
I trust food. I know it will help.
I also know that later
        I will feel guilty about binging
        and have more depression
        because of the extra pounds,
        but right now that seems unimportant.
All I want is the immediate gratification,
        the immediate satisfaction
        of having something in my mouth.
O Lord, give me patience, please.
Help me to ride out this depression,
        to be stronger that it is
        and fight it in creative ways
        instead of with a destructive binge.
Give me strength to tower above these feelings,
        to be in control.
I cannot allow myself to wallow in self-pity,
        for that represents
        neither You nor myself as Your child.
Let Your love flow through me, Father,
        so I can defeat depression
        and sparkle in the radiance of well-being.
Amen.

When Lonely

Father,
I am so alone!
I wonder if even You are here.
Nobody could love me.
I feel useless—insignificant.
No one cares.
People say "how are you" and never listen
      for an answer.
I could reply "dead" as well as "fine,"
      and no one would notice.
Are You here, Father?
Food is here.
I can see it, feel it, taste it.
I can stuff it into my mouth
      until I feel comforted and less alone.
Can You match that, God?
"Lo, *I* am with you always."
What's that I feel?
Not the pity and sympathy I want,
      but a mental kick in the rear.
You are saying to me that being lonely
      is *my* fault!
Why should I take responsibility
      for my loneliness?
Is it because I'm not doing Your work?
If I were doing Your work,
      or if I were doing something for someone
      instead of thinking about myself,
      I wouldn't be lonely, would I?
Father, please forgive
      my lamentations of loneliness

and lead me into creativity and usefulness,
    remembering that You are walking with me.
In Jesus' name. Amen.

Paid for It

But, Lord, I paid for it!
I shouldn't have ordered it, but I did,
    and now it's paid for, so I have to eat it.
Please don't try to confuse me by reminding me
    how much money I've thrown away on fad diets,
    fancy-named placebos,
    and reducing gimmicks.
That's different.
This is food that's been paid for.
But perhaps it *is* worth losing the money involved
    to keep from breaking my diet.
Lord, You give me understanding.
I would pay large sums for a guardian
    to keep me from eating this food.
If I dispose of this temptation,
    I am losing only a few pieces of silver,
    but I gain self-respect, guilt-free conscience,
    pride, and a feeling of control.
What a bargain!
Still, Lord, it is difficult.
Carry for me, Father, the burden of desire
    for this food.
I don't need to eat it just because it's paid for,
    and Lord,
    I won't.
Amen.

Break Time on the Job

Lord,
My diet goes real well
    until that second break of the day.
Then, invariably, I mess up.
If I could stand to stay at my post,
    I would stay just to help my diet;
    but by that time I'm really anxious
    to get out of there and into the break room.
There, for a few cents,
    I find love and comfort in the form of food.
I feel very hungry,
    but—I'm *not really* hungry at second break.
The "hunger" pains are really
    feelings of tiredness and boredom.
I need to cope with these problems
    some way other than eating.
You have given me creativity, Lord.
Help me use it to find something to do on break
    that won't make me fat.
At break I could write a letter,
    or do some exercises,
    or sit with someone interesting.

I can be interested in people instead of food.
Teach me, Lord,
>that I can make it through the second shift
>without stuffing myself.

When I learn I *can* do it,
>it will be easier to continue.

I will be stronger
>and thinner.

Please help me, Father.
We can do it!
Amen.

Considering Snacking

Lord,
I am restless.
I want something in my mouth to chew on.
It's not really hunger, Lord.
I honestly can't say I've ever experienced
>true hunger.

It's just this restlessness and anxiety
>that I habitually interpret as hunger.

Lord, I seek Your peace.
Help me to take a deep breath
>and sit calmly for a minute.

Help me to sort my thoughts
>and overcome this nervousness.

I turn my anxieties and restlessness
>over to You.

I feel my appetite satiated
>by Your loving presence.

I appreciate the stillness of this moment, Lord.
Thank You for granting me Your peace.
Amen.

When Choosing a Snack

Lord,
I really need a nibble.
Please help me choose my snack.
I want to eat right, Lord,
    but even with this desire,
      I sometimes eat whatever is in sight.
Why do I give in so easily
    when I want so badly to defeat this food demon
    that takes control of me?
Help me to create appetizing visual images
    of things that are good for me
    and OK to eat.
Help me to bypass the ever-beckoning diet defeaters
    and see the greasy and sweet little tempters
    as the detroyers they are,
    bringing destruction to my diet,
    my physical well-being,
    and my self-esteem.
Father, grant me the blessing of choosing my snack
    wisely.
Amen.

When Tempted by a Spouse

Lord,
I know my mate loves me.
I also know he recognizes my food weaknesses
    and sometimes appears to be playing the devil,
    teasing and testing.
I want to please by spouse,

and also want his respect.

Each time I yield to one of his temptations,
I cash in some of that respect.
If I don't give in, he reacts angrily,
almost as if he preferred me fat.
Is he afraid
that I will be different with a weight loss
or that our relationship will change?
Does his fear encompass losing me?
Perhaps he thinks I won't want him
when I gain attractiveness.
Lord, help me teach my husband
that the results of my successful dieting
will be good.
By improving and caring for this body,
I please You, respect myself more,
am more content, and am learning to love myself.
The relationship between my spouse and me
will change, I am sure,
but the change will be
toward more encompassing,
fuller loving and caring.
The suspicion and guilt,
intertwined with the food game we play
will disappear and will be replaced
with trust and understanding.
Help me, Lord, with patience
to win my mate's support
and to walk together to the future
in attractiveness and love.
Amen.

When Tempted by Friends

Father,
My friends know I'm dieting,
    and yet they encourage me to eat.
They *know* I'm dieting for the sake
    of my mental and physical health,
    and yet they still make attempts
    to sabotage my diet.
"Oh come on, one bite won't hurt,"
    or "You're wasting away,"
    or "But I made it just for you.
    I know how you like it.
    Don't hurt my feelings by refusing it."
Lord, they really are my friends.
That's what makes it so hard
    to refuse their offers.
I would like my friends to try to understand
    how important this diet is to my well-being.
I would appreciate
    their support and encouragement.
But it's very difficult to find
    this deep understanding.
Lord, I am so grateful You are with me
    in this diet.
Please help me teach my friends
    to understand its seriousness.
If they cannot understand,
    help me reject their temptations,
    and help them realize
    that I am not rejecting them personally.
It is most important that my diet not be subverted.
Love is *not* spelled F-O-O-D.

I can exchange fellowship and affection
     with people without food being involved.
Please give me full awareness of this fact, Lord,
     and walk beside me as I walk with my friends.
Amen.

Lunch Out

Father,
Today I meet with friends for lunch.
I am embarrassed to face them
     and order the diet plate.
What will they think?
How do I conquer this embarrassment?
I must learn that dieting does not mean
     admitting to the world that I am fat.
The world has eyes.

50 Dieting is saying to the world:
          "I appreciate you, world.
          I am going to take care of myself
          and enjoy you with all the senses I possess."
    In You, Lord, I am not weak.
    Dieting is a sign of strength.
    I am proud to be taking care of myself
          and eating as a sane, rational person.
    I am a valuable human being
          given the mind and wisdom to eat wisely.
    Not to use this gift would be wrong.
    Father, help me
          to use the wisdom You have given me
          to eat correctly with pride, not embarrassment.
    I shall hold my head high and see the mountains.
    Thank You, God, for the enlightening perspective
          and insight You have granted.
    Amen.

When Tempted by
Fast Food Restaurants

Lord Jesus,
I drive down any main street and could name it
      "Dieter's Damnation Alley."
The lures are constantly before me:
Odors waft from the grills,
      only 20 minutes for a carry-out.
"Spice up your life with foreign entrees,
      treat yourself to delights"
I deserve a break today — just a quick one — I think.

Fast food in saturated-fat-fried breadings.
If I'm really in a hurry or desperate,
    I can walk or drive under a golden rainbow
    and have food for my mouth
    almost as quickly as I can order it.
I have the fastest hunger in the West.
I see, I want.
This *eye* hunger is dangerous.
Lord, I cannot avoid passing Fast Food Avenue.
Please, teach me to control this appetite
    stimulated by my vision.
When the devil tempted You
    with a vision of wordly glory and pleasure,
    You said to him, "Begone, Satan!"
By the power of Your redeeming love for me,
    help me not to focus
    on quick and easy pacifiers
    for my raging appetite,
    but to look beyond them.
I want to see other things.
Help me defeat
    my obsession with food and restaurants
    so I can see Your world in a normal way.
Let me see the stars.
Amen.

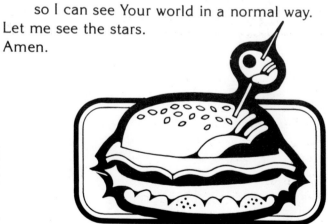

At a Movie

Lord,
Tonight I am going to a movie, and I'm scared.
It's embarrassing to admit this fear,
>   but without recognizing my weakness
>   I can never gather the resources to conquer it.
Today I realized with some astonishment
>   that I have never been to a movie without eating.
I prepare for a show the same way I would prepare
>   for a trek through the desert,
>   gathering rations to refresh and restore.
Often I sit next to an empty seat,
>   not out of shyness or need for isolation,
>   but because I need a place to set
>   my supply of goodies.
I'm afraid to face a two-hour movie without food.
Lord, I need You by my side tonight
>   while I sit through the show.
You can make me aware
>   of the pleasures of seeing a movie
>   without simultaneously stuffing my body.
I can for two hours,
>   without the distraction of food and drink,
>   appreciate fine acting, good photography,
>   and a well-constructed story.
Seeing a movie without food
>   can be an exciting adventure.
Help me, Father,
>   to capture this feeling of adventure
>   and to enjoy this movie and others
>   while on my way to slimness.
Amen.

When Tempted by TV Commercials

Lord,
I watch television
    and desire to be like those "beautiful people"
    that glitter and sparkle,
    the people that so easily find meaning in life
    by drinking the correct soft drink
    or that find love
    through the proper pastries.
You, my Lord, have blessed my life
    with family and friendships
    that give meaning and love to my existence.
Teach me to recognize true values.
Lord, grant me Your truth and wisdom.
Keep me aware of the fantasy
    in the square-boxed view of the world.
Help me to overcome the temptation to let food,
    so tantalizingly disguised as a treat
    or as an answer to my problems,
    be in control of my actions and habits.
Help me also, Lord,
    not to go to the other extreme
    and to make beauty, attractiveness, and thinness
    into gods to be worshiped.
Teach me the blessings of reality
    and of a balanced outlook, Lord.
Amen.

When Fighting Pounds Alone

Lord,
I feel like the only dieter in the world.
I watch others devouring large quantities of food
    and special goodies which I must push away.
I feel like a leper, an outcast, some kind of freak.
I want those things others are enjoying.
I don't want to be different.
I feel so alone.
I have neglected You, Father, when I have problems,
    and have turned instead to sweets for solace,
    foods for friendship,
    and mouth-stuffers for comfort.
You have promised grace sufficient for my needs,
    but instead of seeking Your grace,
    I say grace and stuff my mouth full again.
I turn to You now, Father.
Help me overcome these feelings.
Teach me that I am not alone!
You are with me.
Teach me to not use food
    as the answer to ups and downs in my life,
    but to view food in a realistic perspective,
    enjoying it conservatively.
Help me hang in there Lord,
    and feel Your presence with me.
Halleluia, I am NOT alone.
Amen.

Secret Eating

Lord,
I can't hide from You.
You know about the "goodies" hidden in my dresser,
    in the laundry hamper,
    and under my pillow.
In front of other people
    I eat very carefully and measured.
I would be ashamed and mortified
    if discovered eating secretly.
I don't think I could bear
    the hideous embarrassment of discovery.
To admit that I eat too much to someone else
    would be the pinnacle of shame.
I think no one will ever know
    about my secret eating,
    but whenever I walk out the door,
    I broadcast the evidence of every bite
    I have eaten in secret.
Still, I foolishly delude myself and say,
    "No one will ever know."
Lord, help me stop hoarding food
    like the squirrel gathering his nuts
    before the long winter.
Let me eat in the open
    in moderate amounts without shame.
It's *only food,*
    not my legacy, not my fortune — *only food.*
Those two words
    are hard for me to say together, Father.
Please, keep me in the spirit
    of being able to say *only food.*

56 Food is not to be treated as gold or riches,
      not to be hoarded, not to be worshiped,
      but to be appreciated as Your blessing.
With Your help, Father,
      I will accept and use this blessing
      as You intended.
Amen.

Foodolatry

Lord Jesus,
Why do I eat the way I eat?
Why does food have such a hold on me?
The first bite is always the best,
      and often the only one tasted.
But I never stop with the first bite.
I keep eating
      as if I'm facing Egypt's seven-year famine.

I *want* to eat, but I *don't* want   57
      the consequences of my eating.
True happiness would surely be
      the ability to eat 24 hours a day
      without stomachaches, headaches,
      nausea, or weight gain.
Temperance in all things is a good rule,
      but who *WANTS* to be temperate
      when surrounded by succulent dishes?
Not I.
I want to indulge and pamper myself with food.
My problem, Lord,
      is that I want to eat everything I see or smell.
I have said I would give anything I have to be thin,
      but it is more likely that
      if it were necessary,
      I would give anything I have to get food.
To be thin I don't have to sell my soul,
      cut off my right arm,
      or pay thousands of dollars;
      all I have to do is eat moderately.
But, Lord, as simple as the solution is,
      I can't handle it alone.
I have not been able to control
      my lustful desire for eating.
Please forgive me for my gluttony.
Now please help me change
      my thinking about food.
Help me see that food need not control me,
      that with the Holy Spirit in my heart
      I can use the intelligence You have given me
      to be in control and eat sensibly.
Help me, Lord Jesus.

58 Help me to conquer
the idol my craving for food has become.
With Your help, food will no longer be
my all-consuming passion,
but will become a small pleasure
as it takes its proper place,
providing nourishment
in each beautiful day of my life.
Amen.

When Feeling Forced to Eat

Heavenly Father,
I know I am not hungry,
but I feel a terrible compulsion to eat.
Please, God, help me seek
the source of this compulsion.
What do I really feel that I am calling "hunger"?
Am I sad, lonely, nervous, or depressed?
Help me, Father, to harness
the energies from these feelings
and use them now
for purposes that will honor You.
Lead my hands to creativity.
Let me bless another with a letter
or write a poem
or make something new
or even polish my shoes.
Lead my feet away from the food.
Let me take a walk and appreciate Your blessings—
or maybe even exercise.

Dear Father, help me to become better acquainted
    with my feelings,
      to take control of the compulsion
      that destroys my self-esteem,
      and to know and appreciate myself more.
Help me to see myself as You see me—
      Your forgiven child through Your Son Jesus—
      and to take care of myself
      because You care for me.
Amen.

Fear of Being Thin

Lord,
I don't want to be fat.
You know how I have begged on my knees
      and pleaded in tears with You
      to make me thin,
        to give me the strength to stick to a diet
        for a day—even an hour.
Lord, I want to be thin,
      but every time I lose five pounds I panic.
I am afraid to face the world without fat.
Fat gives me an excuse to be shy and withdrawing.
Fat gives me an excuse to be lazy.
Lord, help me bury these excuses.
You're not forcing me to be fat.
You want me to have self-confidence
      and feel good about myself.
When I step on the scale and see a loss,
      let me view that loss with pride, not panic.

Lord, help me to feel good about myself.
Teach me self-confidence.
I will be thin.
And one step at a time,
      one pound at a time,
      I will learn
      I am a new creature.
Amen.

That Other Sex

Lord God,
Now that I'm losing weight,
      what do I do about the opposite sex?
That's a worry *I've* never had.
If someone finds me attractive, what do I do?
I don't know how to handle a relationship,
      even a *friendship,*
      with a person of the opposite gender.
I've never had any practice
      meeting or talking with *those* people.
I had wrapped a layer of fat around me
      to protect me from that kind of situation—
      a good excuse.
I've always thought of myself as too fat
      to even make contact with the opposite sex,
      much less try to make myself appealing to it.
Father, I have shut out of my life knowing half
      of Your wonderful creation of people
      without even realizing it.
Is the other gender really that frightening?

(I'm a genuine fraidycat
    and have a neurotically enormous fear
    of appearing foolish.
So I've kept myself
    in a fat I've hated and despised
    rather than taking chances
    and risk looking silly.)
Maybe they're just people, too.
After all, You made them as well as me.
I must learn to communicate with the other side.
Father, help me see others as You do.
In Jesus' name. Amen.

Myth: One Bite Can't Hurt

Lord,
One of my biggest diet enemies
    is the "one bite can't hurt" myth.
    I hear it everywhere.
I took "just one bite" at a Christmas party.

Five months, two weeks later, 15 pounds heavier,
crying over swimsuit ads with summer approaching,
I forced myself back on my diet.
I never got a new swimsuit that summer.
When I visit friends and relatives I hear,
"I made it special.
After all that work you could at least taste it."
All right. One taste.
This time I'm off my diet for three weeks.
The "one bite can't hurt" myth seems so logical.
How can one taste of anything make you fat?
It's what it can lead to
that gets you into trouble.
Lord, one bite can keep me from being thin.
As long as I avoid that one bite,
I will continue to shrink.
Protect me, Lord.
Hone my awareness
and help me fight that bite.
Amen.

Encouragement

Lord,
My diet is working.
It's been slow,
but people are beginning to notice.
I'm proud to hear the compliments of my friends.
Flattering remarks boost my spirit
and make it easier to pass up the "no-no's."
It's been with Your help
that these pounds have slipped away.

You hold my hand through the rough times
    and give me a shoulder to cry on.
I have learned to turn to You
    with my problems and feelings
    instead of to food as I once did.
Thank You, Lord, for helping me.
Stay by me as I continue to diet.
Amen.

Seeking Control

Oh, God!
I can't believe I've broken my diet again.
I'm so ashamed.
I *DO* want to be slim, Lord,
    and this is so frustrating.
Each time this has happened,
    I swear I never again will fail.
Why, Lord, does food become
    so obsessively important to me?
Why do I feel such a void,
    then such panic,
    when I see food and think,
    "I can't eat that—it's not on my diet"?
I'm so afraid of not being allowed to eat something,
    that I go ahead and eat it
    just to prove to myself I can have it,
    then often realize I didn't really want
    or even like what I ate.
Am I insane, Lord?
Oh, God, give me an answer!
Restore my sanity.

64   Let me see food with a realistic eye
         and control my feelings about it.
How can I,
      a child of God through faith in Jesus,
      allow myself to be controlled and degraded
      by inanimate morsels of food?
Lord, lift me up.
With Your help, I'm in charge.
I can *choose* to say no to a food
      or to enjoy it without fear or guilt.
Create in me knowledge and awareness
      to use in my fight against temptation
      so I can be the winner.
Food is not, cannot, will not be my master.
Lord, thank You for the blessing of control.
Amen.

Ice Cream Truck

Listen, Lord,
Hear the melancholy tinkle of the bells
    on the ice cream truck sounding in the distance?
The sound awakens my sleeping mouth-hunger
    for something cold and sweet.
Ice cream has long been one of my weaknesses
    when trying to diet.
It is one of my favorite food sensations.
The cold against my tongue,
    the melting seductive way
    it caresses my throat when I swallow,
    the cascade of frozen flavors to choose from—
    all have at one time or another
    contributed to the delinquency of my diet.
But no more, Lord.
The melancholy tinkles trying to lure me
    to the lair that leads to diet destruction
    shall not win today.
Today, with Your help, I am strong.
Today I cannot be seduced
    even by the sweet memories that are so vivid.
Mentally I can taste
    the seducing, sweet, sugary creations
    that tease toward the truck
    delivering dairy delights.
The memories strengthen temptation.
Lord, strengthen my resolve.
The truck passed, and my heart skipped a beat.
But I didn't die.

And I didn't add unwanted calories and carbohydrates
to my already spacious frame.
Now I'm feeling a tingle of pride.
I feel a smile sunshining its way over my face.
The temptation came, *and I didn't give in.*
Thank You, Lord.
Amen.

Learning

Ah, Lord, another day!
I feel so good, my resolve is firm.
My determination to diet successfully is intact.
Now is the time to learn
from my mistakes of the past,
to use the knowledge of why I failed then
to keep me from stumbling today.
This has happened when I have failed
to keep Your peace and love flowing through me
and have allowed myself
to be controlled by external forces.
For instance—I have been in high spirits,
run into someone grouchy, "caught" his mood,
and eaten.
I need to remember
that I am responsible for my feelings.
I have often misblamed another
for my bad emotional state.
Or—I made a mistake.
Instead of correcting the mistake
and forgiving myself,
I ate.

As the food wore off
    and the bad feelings about my error returned,
    I ate more.
I had not completely accepted
    Your blessing of self-forgiveness.
I knew *You* forgave me through Christ,
    but I couldn't forgive myself.
Or—I did something
    that made me feel stupid or embarrassed,
    so I ate.
Eating, Lord, has been my stock answer
    to any emotion I feel—
    even feeling good.
When a "normal" person would laugh or cry,
    I ate.
Father, please, continue teaching me
    to handle my emotions without my food crutch.
Remind me that I have You to lean on.
Teach me that I have laughter and tears.
Even bad happenings can be invaluable
    as growth experiences.
Please give me the emotional and intellectual growth
    without the physical expansion.
Help me to know
    when I reach out for food because of emotion
    and not because of hunger;
    or when I am hiding my feelings from myself
    in a pile of calories
    instead of using the resources
    You have given me to deal with those feelings.
Take my hand, Father, and give it a gentle squeeze
    if it begins to reach for a sweet pacifier.

Walk with me, Father—past the goody shops,
        past the bake sales, past the refrigerator.
Thank You for the glow
        and for the determination I feel now.
Let these feelings strengthen me through the day.
Amen.

Before Sleeping

Father,
Thank You for walking with me through this day.
Help me to evaluate myself,
        my eating, and my actions of the day
        honestly.
If I have failed to walk in Your path
        in my diet or any part of my life,
        please show me ways to make corrections
        so I can live as a child of God.
Bless my sleep so that my body fully rests itself
        and renews its strength.
In Jesus' name. Amen.

Lord,
We've been through much together on this diet.
I know there's still a long way to go,
    but I'm no longer afraid.
When I reached out,
    You took my hand and gave me guidance.
When I fell into the valley of depression,
    You helped me restructure my thinking.
I was able to think positive thoughts,
    see the beauty around me,
    and pass it on.
I reached out to others,
    touched them with the blessings You gave me,
    and crawled out of my own shell of self-pity.
You helped me when I was angry.
I was able to say to You, "Lord, I'm angry."
I expressed my anger
    instead of disguising it with a sweet craving
    or hiding it amid many overly hearty meals.
Now I beat on my pillow
    (which doesn't seem to mind a bit)
    instead of making myself pillow-shaped.
When I got lonely, You said,
    "What's wrong with you?
    Look around and see the need.
    I have work for you to do."
I was able to be a neighbor
    instead of wondering why I had no neighbors.
By the time I could think about being lonely again,
    I wasn't lonely anymore.
When I wanted to quit,

to give up and not fight any longer,
You refreshed my spirit and my enthusiasm.
You helped me not to give in to temptations.
Clearing my vision,
You helped me see through and overcome
my flimsy excuses to break training.
Wisdom was another gift.
I learned to see myself more realistically.
I discovered my worth and value as a person
and as Your child.
I learned I had been using fat
to hide from the world.
With Your guidance, I stepped into reality and
interrelated with people.
My interest in people and my surroundings increased
as my egocentricity diminished.
You helped me learn to deal
with my responsibilities—
to take charge of my life and be in control.
I have put my house in order.
My thinking is clearer.
Excuses to hide from responsibilities
no longer cloud my mind.
My emotions are in tune with the universe.
Food has ceased to be my source of happiness
or the idol I worship.
I can sit through a movie without a doggie bag.
I can walk down the street and see beauty
instead of allowing my soul to lust
for the fast foods around me.
I eat with my friends and enjoy the diet plate.
I use my garbage disposal instead of my stomach.

The scale no longer binds me with its numbers
    or terrifies me.
My energy overflows.
Lord, I can *even* look in a mirror
    and respond to the image I see
    not with self-hate and disgust
    but with a smile.
Thank You, Father.
Thank You for loving me through the fat.
Thank You for believing in me even
    when I couldn't believe in myself.
Thank You for reaching out to me
    though I had doubts, fears, and ran from You;
    for Your touch was followed
    by learning and growth.
Thank You, Father, for keeping me in Your care
    and most especially for teaching me
    that I am Your child through Jesus.
In Him I am OK.
Amen.